90 0751417 9

D1756981

Empathy

Promoting resilience and emotional intelligence for young people aged 7 to 11

**Bob Bellhouse,
Glenda Johnson and
Andrew Fuller**

P·C·P

Paul Chapman
Publishing

ISBN: 1-4129-1159-1

 Published by Lucky Duck
Paul Chapman Publishing
A SAGE Publications Company
1 Oliver's Yard
55 City Road
London EC1Y 1SP

SAGE Publications, Inc.
2455 Teller Road
Thousand Oaks, California 91320

SAGE Publications India Pvt Ltd
B-42, Panchsheel Enclave
Post Box 4109
New Delhi 110 017

www.luckyduck.co.uk

Commissioning Editor: George Robinson
Editorial Team: Mel Maines, Sarah Lynch, Wendy Ogden
Designer: Helen Weller
Cover illustration: Mark Ruffle

First published in Australia in 2004 by Inyahead Press, PO Box 32,
Queenscliff, Victoria 3225. Phone 03 5258 3055, fax 03 5258 3512.
inyahead@iprimus.com.au   www.inyahead.com.au

© Bob Bellhouse, Glenda Johnson, Andrew Fuller 2005

Printed in the Uk by The Cromwell Press Ltd, Trowbridge, Wiltshire.

Kindness is more important than wisdom,
and the recognition of this is the beginning of wisdom.

Theodore Rubin

Lucky Duck is more than a publishing house and training agency. George Robinson and Barbara Maines founded the company in the 1980s when they worked together as a head and as a psychologist, developing innovative strategies to support challenging students.

They have an international reputation for their work on bullying, self-esteem, emotional literacy and many other subjects of interest to the world of education. George and Barbara have set up a regular news-spot on the website at:
http://www.luckyduck.co.uk/newsAndEvents/viewNewsItems
and information about their training programmes can be found at:
www.insetdays.com

More details about Lucky Duck can be found at:
http://www.luckyduck.co.uk

Visit the website for all our latest publications in our specialist topics:

- Emotional Literacy
- Bullying
- Circle Time
- Asperger's Syndrome
- Self-esteem
- Positive Behaviour Management
- Anger Management
- Eating Disorders.

How to use the CD-ROM

The CD-ROM contains a PDF file labelled 'Worksheets.pdf' which contains worksheets for each theme in this resource. You will need Acrobat Reader version 3 or higher to view and print these pages.

The document is set up to print to A4 but you can enlarge the pages to A3 by increasing the output percentage at the point of printing using the page set-up settings for your printer.

To photocopy the worksheets directly from this book, set your photocopier to enlarge by 125% and align the edge of the page to be copied against the leading edge of the copier glass (usually indicated by an arrow).

Contents

Foreword

Can empathy be taught?

The emergence of empathy in a socialised young child is an important right of passage that should be recognised as significant and celebrated with great joy. A newborn baby does not have empathy or behave in an altruistic way – she demands that her needs are met in order to ensure her survival.

The first time she cries for something other than her own needs, maybe the image of a starving child on the television or a dead bird in the gutter, she has taken a great step, necessary for the social behaviours such as sharing, turn-taking and generosity to appear.

Imagine two young children in the playground – one has a bag of sweets and the other has none. We would value the act of sharing but what has to be learned for that to take place? Firstly the boy with the sweets has to be able to imagine the feelings and experience of the child with no sweets. Next, he must have experienced such strong approval for previous acts of generosity that giving a sweet away is a greater pleasure than eating it himself!

So if the child must learn empathy and altruism then the significant adults in her life must consider how to teach her by:

- ▸ modelling the behaviours and explaining them
- ▸ creating opportunities for empathic and altruistic experiences.

The exercises in this publication provide the teacher or facilitator with excellent ideas and resources to achieve this.

Barbara Maines

Director Lucky Duck Publishing

Introduction

Good relationships are not about finding the right person, but about being the right person. The heart of friendship and love lies in empathy and compassion. Buddha once said, 'If you see yourself in others, then whom can you hurt, what harm can you do?'

For children empathy and compassion are habits they can develop, like any other skill. This programme is about empathy, which is a fundamental building block for the positive development and mental health of children. It occurs when one human being has a caring emotional response to another human being or living thing. Empathy is central to our humanity; the development of conscience; love; friendship; and kindness.

To be empathic a child must be able to:

- notice the feelings of another
- understand the feelings of another
- act in a caring way.

Empathy may be demonstrated in many ways, sometimes compassionately, sometimes joyfully and sometimes calmly and quietly. In this sense, empathy is sensitive and kind, both when others are happy and when they are sad.

Empathy develops as children:

- bond, initially with their mothers, and gradually to a broader range of people and other living things
- learn to respect others, through the demonstration of esteem, regard and consideration for others
- begin to understand their feelings.

Empathy is inversely related to aggression, and is a protective factor against aggression. In this sense, the promotion of empathy becomes a preventive strategy against anti-social behaviours like bullying and violence.

Schools promote empathic behaviour when they provide opportunities for children to be with people who help, comfort and share with others.

This Heart Masters teacher resource for primary school-age children is designed to promote empathy. It provides a set of experiential activities, worksheets and reflective questions that encourage young people to explore different elements of empathic behaviour.

Circle Time – Promoting Friendly Behaviour in Circles

Learning about empathy is best achieved when friendly behaviour is evident. While teachers have many different strategies for developing friendly behaviour, we believe sitting students in circles encourages trust, co-operation and shared consideration.

What is Circle Time?

Circle Time is a structured, regular occasion when a class group meets in a circle to speak, listen, interact and share concerns. Circle Time is simple and routine. It provides a forum for students in which they feel comfortable to share and express their thoughts and feelings.

Why use a circle?

The circle is a symbol of unity and co-operation. It indicates that the group is working together to support one another and take equal responsibility for addressing issues and solving problems.

What is the role of the teacher?

Teachers facilitate. They provide a supporting and accepting environment and take part in all activities.

What is the process involved in Circle Time?

The three key elements of traditional Circle Time are:

1. Understanding and valuing myself.
2. Understanding and valuing others.
3. Having positive relationships with others.

How is Circle Time organised?

It is best to allow pupils (whatever age) to sit on chairs, which are placed in a circle with the teacher as part of it. However, if it is necessary for children to sit on the floor each child should have a carpet square. This is not just for comfort; it helps to maintain the circle formation. Everyone needs to be able to see everyone else and be able to establish eye contact.

Circle Time needs to be a planned and regular occurrence – at least once a week.

Having friendly manners

Three friendly manners for Circle Time are:

1. Listening to others.

    Giving each person the right to speak without being interrupted. Allowing everyone to have a turn to speak.

2. Speaking in a friendly way.

    Giving compliments, asking questions and respecting others' rights to their own thoughts and feelings. Avoiding teasing, negative comments and put-downs.

3. The right to pass.

    Giving everyone the right to not speak.

(This explanation is based on: *Circle Time*, Bliss and Tetley, 1993.)

Empathy

Themes

Theme One – Noticing

Activity 1

Purpose

To introduce the idea of noticing differences and change in relation to the feelings of other people.

Preparation

Find the Differences worksheets.

Process

Ask the children to sit in a circle.

Play a 'silent statement' game. Ask the children to stand up and change seats if:

▸ they felt tired when they woke up

▸ they enjoyed their breakfast

▸ they felt happy about coming to school

▸ they feel lazy sometimes

▸ they experience many different feelings in a day

▸ their friends usually notice their feelings

▸ they usually know how their friends are feeling.

Ask the children to complete the Find the Differences worksheets.

When the children have had some time (5 – 10 minutes) ask them to explain the differences between the pictures.

Discuss the different ways children went about noticing difference (for example, concentrating hard, beginning at the top and working downwards, quickly scanning).

Read the following piece twice, each time with different emotions:

1. In a sad way.

2. In a happy way.

Explain to the children the piece is a Ghost talking after receiving an invitation to a birthday party. Each time you read, ask the children, 'How does Ghost feel?'

Ghost's response to Bear's party invitation

> I'm going to my first party ever. I've never been invited to a party before. Children are usually frightened of me. I make them scream. But Bear gave me an invitation. I hope nobody screams.

Brainstorm the different ways you notice the feelings of other people, for example, expressions, tone of voice, what people say.

Discussion questions

Have you ever been upset and nobody noticed?

How did you feel?

Answers to Find the Differences worksheets

Find the Difference – Swimming Fish

1. Starfish at bottom left corner is now black instead of white.
2. Stripes different on large fish at bottom left of page.
3. Fin different on striped fish at top left of page.
4. Missing fin on smallest striped fish.
5. Mouth changed on small fish at bottom of page just above sea plant.
6. Eye changed on small fish at top middle position.
7. Fin shape changed on fish just below the fish changed in No. 6.
8. Extra fish at front of shoal of fish.
9. Fish at front of shoal of fish, right hand side of page, is upside down.
10. Missing seahorse from seaweed at bottom right hand side of page.

Find the Differences – Treasure Chest

1. Cat hair on top of mask.
2. Dog eyes different shape.
3. Starfish missing on dog's left shoulder.
4. Cat mouth different.

5. Eel missing on left hand side of page, near cat's flipper.

6. Turtle pattern different on bottom left hand side of page.

7. Octopus mouth different shape.

8. Piece of pattern missing on bottom of chest.

9. Mouth different on large fish that is swimming into chest.

10. Extra seahorse on right hand side of page near top right hand corner of chest lid.

Activity 2

Purpose

To practise noticing the feelings and behaviour of others.

Process

Explain to students you are going to do a role-play. Depending on the experience of students, consider warm-up activities.

Choose a role-play from those suggested (or develop another idea).

Brainstorm ideas that students might use in the role-play.

Organise students into groups, so they might practise their role-plays.

Players take turns in performing their role-plays.

Discuss these questions:

‣ What happened?

‣ How were the players feeling?

‣ What else might have happened?

Ask the players if they agree with the opinions of the audience.

Role-plays

Everyone should understand that the role-players are playing a role and are not being 'themselves'.

Role-players should volunteer for the task.

Provide sufficient time for the student, or group of students, to develop the character's attitudes and role. Allow time for participants to practise their role before they perform it publicly.

Provide sufficient space to allow participants to conduct the role-play.

Role-players must be treated fairly, not interrupted or distracted.

No-one can be harassed or criticised for the role they play. One way of 'setting boundaries' is to ask students to develop a particular role within a small group, so that the 'player' can be seen to represent the group rather than themselves.

After each role-play, congratulate the players and ask them:

▸ did it go according to plan?
▸ were some aspects more difficult than they expected?
▸ did the role-play end the way they thought it would?
▸ would they do it differently next time?

Role-players must be debriefed or de-rolled after their performance.

De-rolling protects students. The teacher assists the process by explaining that players are not expected to 'be themselves' by a process of formally enrolling and debriefing participants. De-rolling emphasises that they have played a role and have now finished with it. The player can verbally state the role-play is over and that they are no longer that character. They can describe how they felt about the experience and how they might do the role differently next time.

At the conclusion the teacher should thank the students for their co-operation and confirm that the role-play is finished.

Role-play ideas for two players

Lolly Shop

You are in a lolly and ice cream shop. You want to purchase a chocolate ice cream, which is advertised in the window of the shop.

You are a lolly and ice cream shopkeeper who does not have any chocolate ice cream. You cannot admit you do not have chocolate ice cream since you have advertised it in your shop window. You try to interest customers in other flavours, or even some lovely lollies.

Asking Directions

Your wife is about to have a baby. You need to get directions to the nearest hospital. You stop and ask the other player.

Someone stops to ask directions to the hospital. They say their wife is having a baby. For some reason you are convinced they are playing a practical joke. You do not believe their wife is having a baby. So you are determined to expose their practical joke.

Find the Differences –
Swimming Fish

These pictures might look the same, but they have ten differences. Look carefully and see if you can find them.

Draw circles round the differences you find.

Find the Differences – Treasure Chest

These pictures might look the same, but they have ten differences. Look carefully and see if you can find them.

Draw circles round the differences you find.

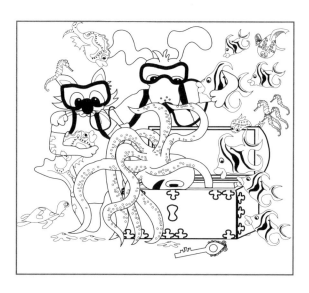

Theme Two – Understanding

Activity 1

Purpose

To compare feelings with other children.

To think about the physical sensations that occur with feelings.

Preparation

Rolls or large sheets of paper.

Felt pens.

Coloured paper.

Process

Arrange the students in groups and ask them to stick large sheets of paper together or to use a roll of paper. Ask one student to lie down whilst the others trace a body outline.

Give students four different coloured pieces of paper (or markers):

1. Red for being 'revved up'.
2. Green for being 'calmed down'.
3. Yellow for being 'cheered up'.
4. Blue for being 'encouraged to think'.

In turns, nominate a feeling from the list and ask children to:

▸ choose a colour (or colours) that each feeling is for them

▸ place the piece of paper on the part of the body where the feeling occurs.

For example: the teacher nominates 'frightened'. A student might choose 'red' because they become 'revved up' when frightened. They might then place the colour on the stomach of the body map to indicate where the feeling is most evident.

Nominate feelings:

Happy	Sad
Angry	Calm
Nasty	Kind
Cruel	Friendly
Frightened	Safe
Lonely.	

In turn, ask students to describe:

▶ where each feeling occurs in the body

▶ what happens to that part of their body.

Discuss whether all students experience feelings in the same way.

Discussion questions

Describe a time when you noticed a person or pet that was unhappy.

How did you feel?

Activity 2

Purpose

To explore feelings.

Preparation

Feelings Without Faces worksheet.

Pencils, crayons and felt tip pens.

Process

Discuss with students the ways people show their feelings:

▶ facial expressions

▶ words and sounds

▶ behaviours.

Ask students to make expressions, sounds or behaviours that demonstrate the following feelings:

angry	worried
helpless	calm
happy	confident
sad	safe
cruel	friendly.

Hand out Feelings Without Faces worksheet.

Ask students to fill in one of the boxes creating a symbol for the feeling; they may use colours, lines and shapes, but not faces.

Share symbols with the rest of the class by explaining why their symbol represents that feeling. The teacher might help students by talking about how dark colours might represent dark feelings and bright colours represent bright feelings. Wave-like shapes might represent rough seas, the sun might represent cheerful feelings and so on.

Ask students to complete their worksheets.

Discussion question

Why are some feelings more difficult to draw than others?

Feelings Without Faces

Create a symbol for the feeling. Use colours, lines and shapes, but don't use faces!

Angry

Worried

Helpless

Calm

Confident

Happy

Sad

Cruel

Friendly

Safe

Theme Three – Acting

Activity 1

Purpose

To consider how students might help others.

Preparation

Dog and Bunji worksheet.

One of the Happiest Days of My Life worksheet.

Pens.

Process

Complete the Dog and Bunji worksheet.

Compare answers.

Ask the students whether they have ever noticed that someone:

▸ brought their new pet to school to show everyone
▸ kept trying to talk but no-one was listening
▸ played really well in a game
▸ said nasty things behind someone's back
▸ spent a lot of time alone in the playground
▸ was home sick from school
▸ achieved something special (for example, climbed the monkey bars)
▸ did not like their present
▸ had a new jacket of which they were proud.

Discuss:

▸ How might they feel?
▸ What might you do to help them?
▸ How might you share their joy with them?

Complete the One of the Happiest Days of My Life worksheet.

Share 'happiest days' with the class.

Discussion questions

Describe a time when you helped a person or pet that was unhappy.

How did you feel?

Activity 2

Purpose

To build on the previous lesson and to remember acts of kindness.

Preparation

Paper and pens.

Process

Ask students about their earliest memory:

▸ How old were you?

▸ What do you remember?

▸ How did you feel?

With students, design a 'life map of kindness'. Don't be too prescriptive regarding the style of the map. It could be a historical lifeline or a geographical style map.

The map shows the journey you have travelled from birth until now.

Along the map, ask students to mark significant events that they can remember. For example: their earliest memory, the day they started school and when they met a special friend.

Now ask students to mark those events they can remember, where they have done something kind for another person or where another person has been kind to them.

Decorate the map.

Empathy

Discussion

Ask volunteers to explain significant events on their maps.

Dog and Bunji

Look at the frames below and put the cartoons into order so the story makes sense. Explain the story.

Using this list of feelings, label each frame with a 'feeling word' that most accurately describes it: calm, happy, angry, nasty, cruel, sad, safe, confident, helpless, scared, kind, friendly, lonely.

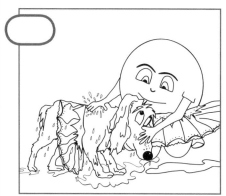

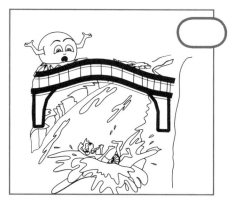

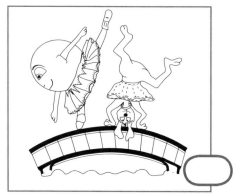

One of the Happiest
Days of My Life

Think about one of the happiest days of your life. Describe why you were happy.

_____

_____

_____

_____

Who shared your happiest day with you?

_____

_____

_____

_____

What did they do to show they were sharing your happiness?

_____

_____

_____

_____

What would your happiest day have been like if nobody had shared it?

_____

_____

_____

_____

Theme Four – Respecting Feelings

Activity 1

Purpose

To think about respecting the feelings of others.

Preparation

Ghost Story worksheet.

Process

Ask the students if they can explain what it means to 'respect someone's feelings.'

Ask the students to form a line. Explain that you will read a statement. If the statement is showing respect for another person's feelings, step to the left. If the statement is not showing respect for a person's feelings, step to the right.

- ▶ taking the biggest piece of cake
- ▶ stopping talking when someone gets a tear in her eyes
- ▶ giving everyone an equal turn in a game
- ▶ bragging about being best at mathematics
- ▶ laughing when someone hurts himself
- ▶ congratulating the winner of the competition.

Read the Ghost Story to the students.

Ask them to complete the story (they could do this in groups).

Compare endings.

Discussion question

How would you feel if people screamed every time they saw you?

NB: Respect involves showing esteem, regard or consideration for another.

Activity 2

Purpose

To explore how people respect others' feelings by making sensitive comments.

Process

Read the following scenarios and answers, and decide which answer would most respect the feelings of the other players.

Discuss:

▸ What happened in each scenario?

▸ How might each response make a student feel?

Difficult sums

One of the other children is having difficulty with their sums. Scratching their head, they say to you, 'I just can't get it.'

a) If at first you don't succeed – give up!

b) It's easy. You must be stupid!

c) Do you want me to try and help?

Losing cards

A student is really disappointed about losing a game of cards.

a) You need to try harder.

b) Having fun is more important than winning.

c) It doesn't matter. It's only a game.

Slow team member

One of your team members is slow in getting their part of a project finished. It is holding everyone up.

a) Do you need any help?

b) Hurry up idiot!

c) How long do you think you will be?

Tough teacher

Another student is complaining that the teacher always gives him the hardest jobs.

a) I agree. The teacher doesn't like you.

b) The teacher must have a lot of confidence in you.

c) Talk to the teacher about it.

Ghost Story

Bear was feeling tired. He had hardly slept in a week. That's how long ago Ghost took up residence in the roof. Of all the houses in the street, Ghost chose Bear's house.

What rotten luck!

The first time Bear saw Ghost, he screamed,

'Aaaaggghhhhhhh Gggggghhhhoooossstttttt!'

And he kept screaming until he noticed that Ghost was upset. Then Bear stopped being frightened and felt pity.

'What's the matter?' asked Bear.

'How would you feel if everyone screamed at you?' said Ghost.

'Aren't Ghosts trying to make everyone scream?' asked Bear.

'No,' said Ghost, 'we've just got a bad reputation. Do you know anyone who has ever been hurt by a Ghost?'

'Come to think of it,' said Bear, 'I don't.'

'See,' said Ghost. 'People are just prejudiced against us. It's rotten being left out all the time, always having to hide in a roof or a basement or a deserted house, only being able to come out in the dark, scaring everybody so much you have to make yourself invisible.'

'Oh dear,' said Bear. 'I never thought I'd find myself feeling sorry for a Ghost. But I am. You can stay in my room if you like and I'll be nice to you.'

'Thanks,' said Ghost.

They were both happy. For a little while…

Until Ghost started making Ghost noises. Bear couldn't understand why. They went on all night…

'Wwwwwoooooooooo! Wwwwwwwooooooooooooooooooo!'

On and on…

Bear couldn't sleep.

He said to Ghost, 'If you don't want to scare people, you shouldn't try to haunt them.'

Ghost protested. 'I'm not trying to haunt anyone. That's just the way a Ghost breathes.'

Oh dear, thought Bear, this is becoming complicated.

And it became even more complicated when Dog and Cat came around to visit.

Guess what they did when they saw Ghost?
Complete the story…

_____

_____

_____

_____

Theme Five – Feeling Compassion

Activity 1

Purpose

To have a brief experience of a difference.

Preparation

Feeling Compassion Raffle Tickets.

Differences and Similarities worksheet.

Pieces of materials with which to tie, blindfold and gag.

Disposable earplugs.

(NB: Ensure the pieces of material have soft edges so they cannot break the skin.)

Process

Ask the children to sit in a circle.

Ask them to turn to the person on their left and to find out:

▸ two similarities they both like (for example, swimming, ice cream)
▸ two differences only one of them likes (for example, football, lettuce).

Take turns around the circle explaining similarities and differences of pairs.

Make up a set of raffle tickets and have clean pieces of material and disposable earplugs.

Raffle Tickets:

▸ Feet tied together, so unable to walk.
▸ Hands tied behind back, so unable to pick anything up.
▸ Blindfolded, so unable to see.
▸ Earplugs in, so unable to hear.
▸ Gagged, so unable to speak.

Explain to the children that you are going to play a series of games. In each game, five children will be limited by a specific difference.

Nominate five students. Distribute raffle tickets. Ask other students to help them tie, blindfold themselves and so on.

Each student should experience a difference for one game of about ten minutes.

Play active games, depending on the age of the students (for example, What's the Time Mr Wolf, Simon Says, Sardines, Three Legged Races).

Complete the Differences and Similarities worksheet.

Discussion questions

What was your difference?

How did it feel?

Activity 2

Purpose

To discuss compassionate behaviour.

Preparation

Compassion Quiz.

Process

Sit in a circle.

Ask the students to complete the quiz.

Discuss the answers.

Discussion question

In each situation, what would be the most compassionate response?

Feeling Compassion
Raffle Tickets

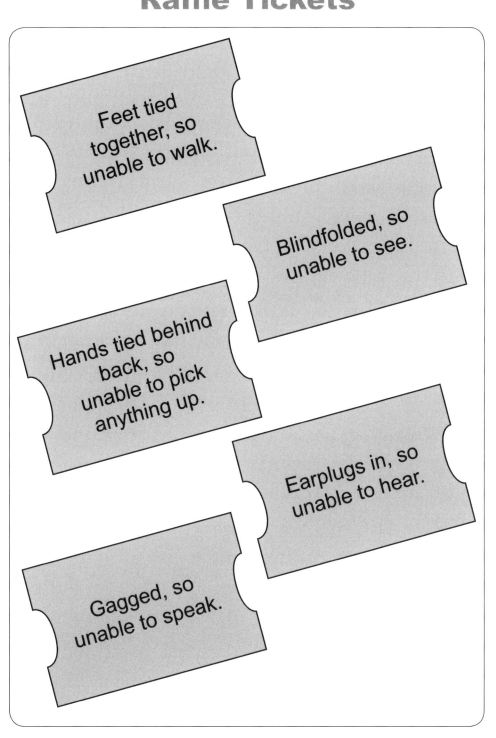

Differences and Similarities

List three ways you are similar to the other children in your class.

_____

_____

_____

List three ways you are different to the other children in your class.

_____

_____

_____

Which people in your neighbourhood might feel different?

_____

_____

_____

How might these people sometimes feel a little left out?

_____

_____

_____

What might you do to help them feel more included?

_____

_____

_____

Compassion Quiz

Tick the answer to each question that describes the way you would respond.

1. Some children in your class are misbehaving for a new teacher.
   Would you:
   a) Quietly do your work ☐
   b) Stand on your desk and dance ☐
   c) Sneak outside ☐
   d) Threaten to punch anyone who misbehaves. ☐

2. A new student comes to your school. Would you:
   a) Play tricks on them ☐
   b) Say 'hello' ☐
   c) Sit next to them ☐
   d) Ignore them. ☐

3. Your mother has been working long hours and has been missing you.
   Would you:
   a) Ask for more pocket money ☐
   b) Complain about her being away ☐
   c) Offer to help with chores ☐
   d) Tell her you love her. ☐

Compassion Quiz continued…

4. Your friend has no money and you want to buy an ice cream.
   Would you:

   a) Not have one ☐
   b) Lend them some money ☐
   c) Wait until they go home ☐
   d) Tell them to get a job. ☐

5. Some students are spreading a nasty rumour about another student.
   It may or may not be true. Would you:

   a) Tell them to stop ☐
   b) Tell the student who is being talked about ☐
   c) Make jokes about it ☐
   d) Join in. ☐

6. Your friend takes your place in a game. They are very excited and
   you are very disappointed. Would you:

   a) Dump them as your friend ☐
   b) Ask them not to be so happy ☐
   c) Try and feel happy for them ☐
   d) Explain how disappointed you are. ☐

Theme Six – Bonding

Activity 1

Purpose

To explore how people bond with other people or living things.

Preparation

Pets worksheet.

A hard-boiled egg for each student.

Material for making comfortable containers for their eggs.

Paints.

Process

Form a circle.

Ask the children to complete the sentence:

'My favourite pet is...'

Complete the Pets worksheet.

(NB: If a student does not have a pet, they might like to write about a pet they would like to have, or someone else's pet that they are fond of, or even help another student write about their pet.)

Bonding with an Egg

Give out hard-boiled eggs to each student. Explain that they are very precious, and that each of them is responsible for their egg for a week. Their challenge for one week is to:

▸ Keep their egg safe.
▸ Keep the egg with them at all times.
▸ Keep their egg comfortable.
▸ Talk to their egg.
▸ Be kind to their egg.

Ask the children to:

- give their egg a name
- paint a face on their egg
- Make a comfortable container (bed) for their egg.

Ask the children to keep a diary of the week with their egg and to describe:

- what they did with their egg
- how they felt.

Discussion questions

Describe how you feel about your egg.

Share experiences and feelings, for example:

- if the egg's shell was broken, discuss feelings about responsibility
- whether feelings changed over the week
- whether any students will miss their egg.

Activity 2

Purpose

To encourage students to think about whom they might trust and from whom they might seek support.

Preparation

Wise Guide worksheet.

Process

Ask the students who they would seek help from if they:

- needed some medicine because they were ill
- could not do their schoolwork
- had a problem that was private
- were really worried about something
- felt sad.

Discuss questions.

Explain the Wise Guide worksheet and ask the students to complete.

Discussion questions

Why do people seek help from different people?

Why do people often have a special person with whom to talk?

What are the most important qualities in a person from whom to seek guidance?

Variation

Teachers could make the characteristics, qualities and skills into cards and distribute to students. Then they could have a continuum activity where students place their card along the continuum in response to the question, 'How important is the word in your card when choosing a person to confide in?'

Pets

Describe your pet.

_____

_____

_____

_____

Explain how you care for your pet.

_____

_____

_____

_____

What is your favourite game you play with your pet?

_____

_____

_____

_____

Explain whether your pet is like a friend.

_____

_____

_____

_____

How do you think your pet feels about you?

_____

_____

_____

_____

Wise Guide

What characteristics (older, same age, male, female, friend, family, religious) and qualities (trustworthy, kind, generous, friendly, funny, calm, listener, thinker, experienced, wise) do your Wise Guides have?

	Characteristic	Quality
Need medicine		
Can't do homework		
Private problem		
Worried		
Sad		

What do you think are the most important characteristics?

1 _____

2 _____

3 _____

What do you think are the most important qualities?

1 _____

2 _____

3 _____

Theme Seven – Helping

Activity 1

Purpose

To introduce the idea of philanthropy.

Preparation

Access to the Internet or home preparation by students to gather information.

Process

Set a project where students identify a charity, local community group or philanthropic organisation that helps people.

Ask the children to write letters, surveys or search the internet to find out about the organisation:

▸ What does it do?

▸ How was it started?

▸ How does it help people?

▸ How does it make a difference?

Ask the students to present their information about their organisation to the class.

Extension activity

Some teachers and students may wish to choose an organisation to support.

Talk about how the class might support the organisation:

▸ volunteer work

▸ promotion

▸ fund raising.

Make a plan and allocate roles.

Discussion questions

What would happen if nobody supported charities?

Why do so many people care about people they have never met?

Activity 2

Purpose

To practise thinking about others and ways of helping.

Preparation

Helping Game worksheet.

Pens and dice.

Process

Form students into groups.

Hand out Helping Game worksheet and a dice.

Explain the game.

Instructions

▶ Roll the dice four times, circling a square in each row according to the number you roll. For example, if you roll number two with your first roll, you would circle, 'Picked on by older students'. If you roll three with your next roll, you would circle, 'Enjoys playing sport'. And so on...

▶ When you have rolled the dice four times, write down the profile of your person and complete the rest of the Helping Game worksheet:

Guess whether the student is male of female.

Give the student a name.

Describe the student and their problem.

Suggest ways the group might help their student.

Helping Game

Roll the dice four times circling a square in each row according to the number you throw.

Write down the profile of your person and complete the questions.

	Problem	Favourite thing	Friends	School
1	Left out of games	Television	Hangs out with older tough kids	Gets bored easily
2	Picked on by older students	Shopping	Always changing	Tries at most things
3	Gets into trouble with teachers	Playing sport	One close friend who recently moved away	Has a special talent
4	Changing schools	Being cheeky	Seems to normally have lots.	Complains a lot
5	Strict parents	Dancing	A loner	Finds schoolwork difficult
6	Pet died	Skating	No close friends, but not unpopular	Enjoys most things

What is the profile of your person?

_____

_____

_____

_____

Guess whether the student is male of female.

Give the student a name.

Describe the student and their problem.

Suggest ways the group might help their student.

Theme Eight – Sharing

Activity 1

Purpose

To reflect on the joy of sharing.

Preparation

Sharing worksheet.

Pens.

Preparation of dishes by students at home – ask all the students to prepare their favourite dish at home and to bring it to school (or students could design a class menu and ingredients could be purchased by school and prepared in class).

NB: A variation on this activity could be for students to bring their favourite game to play with the other students, to share their favourite story, or music and so on.

Process

Ask each student to 'pass a smile' (squeeze, compliment, wink) by turning to their right and smiling. The next student receives the smile and passes it on around the circle.

Discuss:

How does it feel to share a friendly expression or touch with another person?

Brainstorm a list of the things people share.

Discuss questions.

Complete the Sharing worksheet.

Ask each student to present his or her favourite dish to the class, explain how it is prepared and describe:

▸ the taste sensations

- ‣ how often they eat it?
- ‣ whether it is a family favourite.

Ask the students to then share their favourite dish among the class.

Discussion questions

How do you feel when you share with others?

How do you feel when others share with you?

Activity 2

Purpose

To explore the idea of sharing and being thoughtful when having fun.

Preparation

Good Sports Report Card.

Pens and paper for posters.

Board games.

Process

Select games (board games, active team games and so on).

Play games with students.

Once students have completed their games, ask them to fill out the Good Sports Report Card.

Form students into pairs.

Now ask students to fill out a Good Sports Report Card for their partner. Compare report cards to see how similar they are.

Brainstorm the personality traits that make games enjoyable for everyone.

Discuss questions.

Make up posters with positive messages to place around the classroom.

Discussion questions

When do you enjoy games the most?

Do you enjoy games when you don't get much of a turn?

Do you enjoy games when you get more turns than other players?

Sharing

List some of the things you share with others.

_____

_____

_____

_____

_____

_____

How do you feel when you share with others?

_____

_____

_____

_____

_____

_____

List some of the things others share with you.

_____

_____

_____

_____

_____

_____

How do you feel when others share with you?

_____

_____

_____

_____

_____

_____

Good Sports Report Card

Tick the boxes that show how you behaved in your game.
Ask a friend to tick the boxes that describe the way they think you behaved.

Quality	What I think	What my friend thinks
Funny		
Honest		
Determined		
Sharing		
Creative		
Angry		
Friendly		
Leader		

Theme Nine – Comforting

Activity 1

Purpose

To think about giving comfort to others.

Preparation

A Secret Friend Ticket for each student.

Materials to make cards.

Process

Form a circle.

Talk about the ways people give each other comfort in families.

Ask students to complete the sentence:

'When someone in my family comforts me I feel…'

Discuss why people send each other cards.

Make Secret Friend Tickets, one for each student.

Ask each student to draw a ticket and to keep their ticket secret.

Explain that the task is to design a 'friendship card' for their secret friend. They should put their 'friend's' name on the front of the card and draw a portrait of them, or another picture that represents their friend. Then they find three people to write compliments (or things they like or appreciate) about the person.

When the cards are complete, take turns in presenting the cards to each student. The 'designer' explains their picture on the front of the card, and reads out the compliments.

Discussion questions

How do compliments give people comfort?

Describe a time when you have comforted another person or a pet.

How do you feel when you give a person or pet comfort?

Activity 2

Purpose

To show how you might comfort others by talking with them.

Process

Form a horseshoe.

Place a 'Likely' sign at one end of the horseshoe and an 'Unlikely' sign at the other end.

Ask students to stand along the continuum according to the likelihood of an event. Read out one 'Worrying Event' at a time:

getting picked on

being attacked by terrorists

failing a test

having no friends

getting an incurable disease

coughing into someone's face

parents divorcing

the bus being late

being struck by lightening

being in a car accident

being kidnapped by aliens

getting dog poo on your shoe

losing something precious.

Ask students to explain why they are standing in a certain position. Where relevant, teachers might add additional questions. If this event happened:

▸ What is the worst possible outcome?

▸ What is the best possible outcome?

▸ What is the most likely outcome?

Discuss these questions.

Brainstorm things students worry about.

(NB: ask students to not reveal anything that is too personal.)

Set up a panel of experts (volunteers). Ask the other students to write down anonymous worries, fold them and place them in a box. The experts select 'worry scenarios' from the box and discuss them by predicting:

▶ the worst outcomes
▶ the best outcomes
▶ the most likely outcomes.

Discussion question

How might you use what you have learned in this lesson to help comfort a friend?

Theme Ten – Circle of Kindness

Purpose

To encourage kind behaviour.

Preparation

A story about kindness.

Sheet of paper per student.

Paint for self-portraits.

String.

Strips of paper.

Stapler.

Process

Read a story to students about kindness or talk about kind acts.

Ask students to think of a time when:

‣ someone has been kind to them
‣ they have been kind to someone.

Brainstorm a list of kind (generous, friendly, thoughtful) acts.

Discuss questions.

Ask each student to draw a large self-portrait.

Place the self-portraits at equal distances around the class.

Ask the students to record, onto strips of paper, all of the kind, generous and friendly acts they can remember that they have done, or someone has done for them, in the classroom. They might form into groups or pairs to complete this task.

Join the strips of paper on pieces of string long enough to connect the hand of one portrait to another. (Staple or tape together.)

Throughout the year keep adding strips until all the students are joined by acts of kindness, generosity and friendship in a circle.

Discussion questions

How do you feel when you are kind to another person?

How do you feel when someone is kind to you?

If you practise being kind, do you get better at it?

Developmental Work

Empathy is such an important aspect of an emotionally literate person that we must continually provide the opportunity for young people to develop this essential human quality.

As well as provide the opportunities adults must model empathetic behaviours. They can also look at developing a school ethos where empathy is an essential element.

The following ideas provide some exercises that will encourage young people's empathic responses.

1. Put all class members names in a hat. Ask each student to draw out a name. Ask them to design a friendly postcard and write some friendly comments for the person they drew out of the hat. Collect the postcards and post them for the students.

2. At the end of each day ask the students to sit in a circle and express an appreciation about another. Remember, students have a right to pass.

3. Ask the students to pick names out of a hat. Without telling whose name they have, they do something positive for that person each day for a week. At the end of the week, ask the students to guess their positive supporter.

4. Break students into pairs. Ask each pair to identify a positive attribute they share in common. Report back to the class.

5. Ask a student to sit in a thank you chair. Ask each student to line up and, one at a time, thank the other student for something.

6. On Valentine's Day collect valentine messages for each student. If one or two names are missing, make a message up. Read the messages out to the class.

7. Design a set of posters with empathic logos and drawings. Display them around the school.

8. Read stories and guess the feelings of the characters. Ask the students to provide evidence for their guess. Evidence might include expressions, thoughts and behaviours.

9. Play an active game. At the end of the game discuss the range of feelings students experienced during the game (excitement, anticipation,

irritation, determination). Compare the difference in feelings among students.

10. Watch a movie or piece of television with the students. Stop the programme at different points and ask them to record how they are feeling at each point. Compare feelings at the end of the programme.

11. Discuss emotions and feelings when reading stories and doing other language-based activities.

12. After playing games, debrief about the children's feelings.

13. During student/parent meetings, talk about how the child and parents are feeling about school, as well as different subjects or activities.

14. When talking about a child's artwork, talk about the feelings being portrayed and how the artwork makes the audience feel.

15. Make posters with children expressing feelings to put around the classroom.

16. Ask children about their feelings when discussing their behaviour. For instance, if a child is complaining about another child's behaviour, rather than asking about the behaviour, ask the complainant how they feel. If following up an incident with another child, once again, rather than concentrating on the behaviour, explain how the complainant is feeling.

17. Select a variety of pictures, cartoons or artwork that are:

   ‣ appropriate to students
   ‣ likely to evoke a variety of emotional responses.

   Discuss:

   ‣ How does each picture make you feel?
   ‣ Do you have more than one feeling about some pictures?
   ‣ Why do people sometimes have different feelings about the same event?

Bibliography

Bliss, T. & Tetley, J. (1993) *Circle Time*, Lucky Duck Publishing: Bristol.

Fuller, A. (1998) *From Surviving to Thriving: Promoting Mental Health in Young People*, Australian Council for Educational Research: Melbourne.

Goleman, D. (2003) *Destructive Emotions; and how we can overcome them*, Bloomsbury: London.

Goleman, D. (1996) *Emotional Intelligence*: Bloomsbury: London.

Resnick, M.D., Harris, L.J. & Blum, R.W., (1993) The impact of caring and connectedness on adolescent health and wellbeing, *Journal of Paediatrics and Child Health*, 29 (Suppl. 1), S3-S9.

Seligman, M. (1993) *What You Can Change and What You Can't: Learning to Accept Who You Are*, Random House: USA.

Seligman, M., Reivich, K., Jaycox, L. & Gillham, J. (1995) *The Optimistic Child*, Random House: Australia.

Thompson, K.L. & Gullone, E. Promotion of Empathy and Pro-social Behaviour in Children through Humane Education, *Australian Psychologist*, Vol 38, No.3, Nov, 2003, Monash University: Australia.